THE WALK

A Moment in Time
When Two Lives Intersect

MICHAEL CARD

THOMAS NELSON PUBLISHERS
Nashville

Published in Nashville, Tennessee, by Thomas Nelson, Inc.

Scripture quotations are from the HOLY BIBLE: NEW INTERNATIONAL VERSION®. Copyright © 1973, 1978, 1984 by International Bible Society. Used by permission of Zondervan Publishing House. All rights reserved.

Library of Congress Cataloging-in-Publication Data

Card, Michael, 1957–

    The walk : a moment in time when two lives intersect / Michael Card.

      p. cm.

    ISBN 0-7852-7750-1

    1. Card, Michael, 1957– 2. Lane, William L., 1931– 3. Christian life. I. Title.

BR1725.C2357 A3 2001

277.3'082'0922—dc21   00-051957

  [B]   CIP

Printed in the United States of America

1 2 3 4 5 6 BVG 06 05 04 03 02 01

Dedication

~ THIS BOOK IS dedicated to Brenda Lane. Had you not been so generous and open to sharing Bill with me and so many others, our walk might have never even begun.

Contents

APPENDIX ～

Acknowledgments

~ Again, I would like to thank Brenda for encouraging me to go to Bill and ask for a block of time all those years ago and more recently for working meticulously through this manuscript.

The men of the Empty Hands Fellowship stood with Bill during those final difficult months, offering their badly needed support and prayers. I joyfully remain forever in your debt.

Michael Podesta, whose poem "IMAGINE" is quoted in this book. His cards and pictures can be ordered from him at 8847 Eclipse Drive, Suffolk, VA 23433 (telephone number 1-800-922-3595).

Finally, I would like to acknowledge my wife, Susan, my partner in an even more significant and longer lasting walk. "God made marriage before He made ministry," a very wise man once said. Without you, neither would be conceivable for me.

He will walk beside us
A strong friend, Barnabas.
He will be the sure shoulder to lean on.
The promise we share
Is our burden to bear,
And our Light tells the darkness to be gone.

He will come after me,
This young Timothy,
Looking for someone to guide him.
I will kindle his Light.
Make him strong for the fight.
I will promise to be there beside him.

The great need of us all,
A true mentor, a Paul
Who has traveled the road that's before us.
He has made good the pledge
To take the Light on ahead.
We can follow his footsteps before us.

FROM "BEARERS OF THE LIGHT."
WORDS BY MICHAEL CARD. COPYRIGHT © 1994
BIRDWING MUSIC. ALL RIGHTS ADMINISTERED BY EMI
CHRISTIAN MUSIC GROUP.

Preface

ORIGINALLY BILL LANE and I committed to write a book together about the discipling relationship. Over the course of five or so years, we met and talked about it, swapping notes on the subject and developing our outline.

After Bill and his wife, Brenda, made their move to Franklin, we supposed we would have plenty of time to work together on the project. But such was not the case. Certainly we had more frequent discussions on the topic, but as Bill's health deteriorated, the project was put on the shelf so he could focus more intently on spending time with his loved ones and those of us who were privileged to walk with him during those final, difficult, and wonderful days.

On one of those last days, he looked regretfully at me and said, "You're going to have to write the discipleship book on your own."

I remember muttering something like, "No, we still have plenty of time to finish it."

But we both knew that wasn't true.

When I finally set to work on the project, I had almost two hundred pages of our notes, mostly Bill's academic observations on discipleship as a "subject." What happened then was one of those wonderful "coincidences" only God can arrange.

My best friend had been given a little book called *Tuesdays with Morrie* by Mitch Albom. After reading it he passed it on to me saying, "This sounds a lot like your experience with Dr. Lane."

I read Albom's amazing book in one sitting and was tremendously moved by the way his experience with his own mentor paralleled mine in so many ways. That book helped me realize that the journal entries about my experiences with Bill might become the frame around his more academic material on discipleship. After all, Bill's life had been the frame that surrounded and validated his own teaching.

So the book you hold in your hands is both a study and a journal. The journal is the frame, the lived-out experience of the study, a reconstruction of our years together, which contains primarily my memories and some ideas we discussed together before Bill went home to be with the Lord. The study from the life of Jesus is the foundation Bill provided from one of his lectures, "The Cycle of Discipleship."

The rabbinic literature we know as the Talmud is divided into two major sections. One of these is called the *Halachah*. It is a Hebrew word that means "walk" and is composed of laws and regulations and all the relevant discussions and opinions of the rabbis. The other division is the *Hagadah*, or "stories." In rabbinic terms then, this book is both *halachah* and *hagadah*. It is composed of stories, as well as teachings, about discipleship. But it should be pointed out that the walk always comes first.

> *Walk* before me and be blameless.
>
> GENESIS 17:1

PART I

The Concept

The Ways and Means of Discipleship

⌒ THE CHRISTMAS SEASON was always a special time for our little community at Western Kentucky University in Bowling Green. At Cecelia Memorial Presbyterian, the small biracial church where my mentor Bill Lane was "interim" pastor for about ten years, we usually had a unique service with carols, new songs, candles, and a message from Bill.

I remember one Christmas especially well. It was 1987. There had been a more than adequate snowfall. Those of us who were responsible for the music had done our best to prepare for the evening. Bill showed up, uncharacteristically, in a flannel shirt his wife, Brenda, had given him as an early present. He sat between my friend Chuck Beckman and me and bellowed "Silent Night" in a key that was ridiculously high for him (but perfect for us).

Later during the service, Bill spoke from the nativity passages of the Gospels. He was sitting in a chair on the empty platform bathed in the spotlight that was usually focused on the pulpit. In that setting he drew our attention to the mystery of the Incarnation.

"When God gives a gift, He wraps it in a person," he said. No high-powered theology, no Athanasian Creed or formal statement of faith. Bill had wrestled with the text of Scripture and was now giving us a new gift of understanding: the Incarnation as a gift. Jesus as a present that you unwrapped for Christmas—what a wonderfully new idea!

Of all that makes our faith unique and true, one feature especially stands out: the Incarnation of Jesus of Nazareth. If you are truly a believer in the biblical sense of the word, you believe that Jesus is God "in the flesh," which is what the word *incarnation* means. When God sought to speak the truth to mankind, He spoke a living Word (Heb. 4:12), and the Word became flesh (John 1:14). Jesus' sacrifice was ultimately sufficient because it was a "living sacrifice." And so we are commanded to offer our own bodies as "*living* sacrifices." We who are His *living* stones walk a *living* way alive with a *living* hope. But it does not end there.

The Incarnation expresses itself at every level of Christian experience. This is seen in a peculiar habit of most of Jesus' followers. So many times, when we are trying to express the truth ourselves, we invariably resort to pointing to a person or telling a story.

"It is like . . ." we stammer, and then proceed to tell a story about someone we know and how the truth came alive in them.

For example, when speaking about the faithfulness of God in our lives most of us will end up telling a story about a time in our own experience—or that of someone else—when God demonstrated himself to be faithful. The reason we so often do this is that our faith is essentially incarnational. It is "fleshed out" in our experience, which is another way of saying it is real.

I would like to speak to you now about discipleship. I could do so in technical, academic words that would bore us both to death. Instead, I will do what Christians from the beginning have done—I will tell you a story because something as important as discipleship cannot be reduced to a definition or contained in a program. The truth of it must be lived out to be properly understood. It is organic; it flexes and moves and defies definition. That is the *way* of discipleship.

The *means* of discipleship is, to use an excessively big word, peripatetic. Which is a fancy way of saying it involves a walk. Discipleship is essentially a walk that two people share together over the course of months or, hopefully, years. It is in the context of the walk that the truth becomes fleshed out and alive. We see the truth of this in the life of Jesus. (You see, we invariably point to a person!)

We could say that the four Gospels are the story of a walk. (This is especially true of Luke, whose great central section—from chapter 9, verse 51 to chapter 19, verse 27—is the story of Jesus' final walk to Jerusalem.) The means Jesus used to disciple those He had called was to walk with them, figuratively as well as literally, for the two and a half to three indescribably precious years they spent together.

My story is about a walk that lasted for twenty-five years and who knows how many thousands of miles. The person I would like to point to, who incarnated so much of the truth for me and countless others, is William L. Lane. And, of course, in the process of pointing to him, I will always be seeking ultimately to point to Jesus. This book is not a program, nor does it seek to exhaustively define all that discipleship means. It is simply a story. Our story.

"When God gives a gift, He wraps it in a person," Bill Lane said. The true purpose of giving a gift is that in the giving, we give a part of ourselves. And so it is with God, the greatest of givers. The special people He gifts us with are another way He gives us Himself.

What a gift Bill Lane was to me and to so many others. Not simply because of the giving of himself, but most especially because he helped us all to unwrap just who Jesus is and what He means. To help others unwrap Jesus—what a superb definition of discipleship!

"I walk with a purpose."

The first thing I noticed about Bill was his walk. Every day, at precisely the same time, he would walk past my Hebrew class. I use the word walk *because I know of no other word that describes his gait. It was not quite a march, though the steps had the force of a march. It was not a run, though one click more and it might have rightly been called that.*

I could hear his steps coming down the hall—quick, rhythmical taps. Then he would flash past the doorway. In that instant I would glimpse a stocky man of average height, his already graying hair with bushy, muttonchop sideburns. His head was always tilted slightly downward, his glasses usually riding halfway down his nose, as if he were about to run through a brick wall. My impression was that if he decided to, he would win out over the wall every time!

Behind his glasses flashed quick, smallish gray eyes. The wrinkles that were beginning to form around them were in the shape of his habitual smile. Above them were two bushy eyebrows that naturally grew straight up. What a picture he presented, a "character"—and God help anyone who might wander into his path!

Later, after we began walking together regularly, he would say, "I walk with a purpose," which was his way of expressing that his ridiculous pace was difficult for someone to keep up with, even a person thirty years younger. I decided he walked with a purpose because he always seemed to know exactly where he was going. Somewhere deep inside himself he sensed an urgency to "get on with it." His walk was a parable of his life and, through him or because of him, it would become the parable of my life as well. It was because of Bill's sense of purpose that I had the privilege of walking with him literally and figuratively for the next twenty-five years.

It is impossible to estimate the value of that first moment when two lives intersect, or to determine the myriad circumstances that had to have been just so in order for one person to meet and come to know another in any given space in time. Our lives connected on a glorious fall mid-morning in 1975 on the third floor of Cherry Hall at Western Kentucky University. I initially came there pursuing a degree in wildlife management. The great vision I had for my life was to someday do bird counts for the Forestry Service.

When my high school guidance counselor asked me, "What is your first priority for a job?" I had answered,

"That it not involve people." My favorite quote in those days was from Sir Thomas More: "Whenever I have gone into the world of men, I have always returned less a man than I was before." Little did I know that I would meet a man who would compel me by his own life and sense of purpose back into the world of people, for Jesus' sake.

The circumstances that brought Bill to Western were painful: a divorce and subsequent exclusion from a theological school where he'd been a professor. At this moment in his life, his theological degree from Harvard could not earn him a job anywhere, "even as a garbage man," he would sometimes say, with a twinge of humiliation in his voice. As I think about it, he often spoke about humiliation.

But then Ron Nash, the kind and courageous head of the religion department at Western, gave Bill an invitation, first to teach religion and Latin part-time. (Latin was only one of fourteen languages he spoke.) Eventually, he would teach New Testament as well as Jewish and Hellenistic backgrounds in the religion department.

Bill had arrived at Western only the year before we met. My Baptist background had conditioned me to be wary of the professors who might seek to tear my faith apart and then leave me to my own devices to piece it back together. I was warned by my elderly Bible teacher to guard myself against people like Bill who were so well schooled, they could win any biblical argument whether their position was true or not.

In essence, I had been given the notion that truth is so frail and fragile, it needs to be sheltered and protected from those who would seek to shatter it with untruth.

Instead, Bill would introduce me to the Truth that can stand on its own against the gates of hell itself. This Truth does not shackle a person to a lifetime of defending and protecting it. Instead, this Truth sets us free.

As the echo of the clip-clop of those determined footsteps died away down the hall, I asked myself, Who is this guy anyway? *For years to come I would be gathering bits and pieces of the answer.*

Those of us who were together at Western still refer to those college days as "the golden years." They were golden for two reasons. First, practically everything that can be good about being nineteen and in college was happening to me. I was free to pursue any subject that interested me, and for the most part, my professors were all men and women who loved the subjects they taught. But golden also because, with Bill's help, I was awake and alive to how good it was, all while it was happening around and in me.

After all, that's one of the tasks of the discipler, to wake us up to what is really going on around us, to encourage us to take our eyes off ourselves and see that our world is not the only world. That outside the narrow confines of the self there exists a world that truly is golden. And they allow us to borrow their eyes until we can see it for ourselves.

"Timing is of the Lord."

⌒ **FROM BILL:**

I first discovered the joy of close friendships with students as a seminary professor. Who would take these students' place when I left the seminary for the secular environment of a state university? I often wondered. That question had to be faced when I accepted an appointment as Professor of Religious Studies at Western Kentucky University. I prayed that God would bring into my life young men who were open to developing a relationship with me and who could be challenged for Christ.

I had an intimate understanding of the benefits of mentoring. My senior colleague at Gordon-Conwell Seminary, Dr. Glen Barker, had invested more than two hundred hours with me, teaching me by example the art of providing guidance to a willing heart. And I had spent the previous fifteen years mentoring many young men myself.

Once I relocated to Western Kentucky, the courses I taught in biblical studies and Jewish and Hellenistic backgrounds to the New Testament gave me a broad exposure to students.

"Have you met your young man yet?" my wife, Brenda, would ask. I'd smile and say, "Not yet, but timing is of the Lord," knowing that I had imposed a condition on my prayer. The young man I was seeking would have to take the initiative and ask for a block of time with me. I was confident that God would prompt a few to do so.

I first met Michael in my Life of Paul class. He was simply one of perhaps twenty-five students who began to be gripped by Paul and the radical character of his missionary vision. The quality of Michael's questions alerted me that he was bright and eager to learn. His paper on Paul and Pharisaism gave us both a chance to talk seriously about the work we shared in class and for me, particularly, an opportunity to learn something of the young man, not simply the student.

Although I can't recall the circumstances that led us to begin to walk and talk together, this experience became the high point of my week at the university for five years. Michael declared a religion major and began studying under my direction, first as an undergraduate, then as a graduate student. Our work in the classroom was enhanced by our growth in relationship as men who were prepared to listen to each other and to be honest with each other.

I had accepted responsibility for the leadership of a small congregation that soon became biracial. Soon Michael began fellowshipping with us as one of a growing number of university students who were seeking a teaching ministry. When I began that work, the church membership was only thirteen, and we sang a cappella *because no one could play the piano or an instrument. Gradually, gifted students joined us and began to respond creatively to the ministry of preaching. Consequently, we enjoyed original music nearly every Sunday.*

Michael was particularly gifted among the musicians God loaned to us. He could play anything with strings— piano, guitar, banjo, dulcimer—with ease, and the songs he composed were biblically rich and engaging.

On one of our walks, I recall asking him to write a chorus for our congregation, based on the sermon for that week. The three points of the sermon became a verse and a chorus, a pattern Michael adopted as his own. One Sunday morning following Easter, I remember preaching on John 21. The next Tuesday I found on my desk the lyrics for "Stranger on the Shore," a song which was later released on Michael's first album, First Light.

It is now impossible to separate the man and the former student I knew in those early years from the contemporary Christian artist and spokesman for compassion for the destitute. My dominant impression of those times is of the joy of our walking and talking together each week. Michael was struggling with godly manhood, and he was hungry to learn. I was open to discuss any topic Michael chose—whether it was women or Scripture. We were almost unaware of the strength of the friendship the Lord was forging through shared study, worship, and ministry. I felt honored by God who gave me the gift of a son wrapped in the person of Michael concurrently with the gifts of lyric and song.

With Michael I've seen music facilitating worship and informing everyday life. His music is a response to the rich legacy God has left us in His Word, and especially in the Incarnation. Theology is always expressed in song before it becomes frozen in refined statement. I thank God for the privilege of being the water that primed Michael's pump, that together, by God's grace, we may extend a cup of cold water in Jesus' name to a thirsty generation.

～ FROM MICHAEL:

I honestly don't know how the idea first came to ask Bill for a block of time. Perhaps I had heard him telling someone else about it. Anyway, one morning I nervously approached Brenda, Bill's lovely wife, who was the secretary of the Religion Department.

"Do you think Dr. Lane might be able to give me some time?" I sheepishly asked.

"Why don't you go ask him," she said with a mischievous smile that I would not understand for another ten years.

Go and ask him! I thought. It was like going into the lion's den. Would I interrupt him? Might he be working on some important paper or book?

I proceeded to his office door, knocking as softly as humanly possible, half hoping that he would be so absorbed in what he was reading or writing that he would not hear.

"Come!" answered a booming voice.

I opened the door to reveal a long, narrow office. It was almost a hall. The walls were lined with bookshelves that went all the way to the ceiling. Upon those shelves books were solidly packed, with volumes lying horizontally on top of the verticals. Each book was bristling with three-by-five cards, which were tucked throughout the pages and covered with his indecipherable scribbling. ("You must learn to interact in the margins of your books," he always said. "That way you can pull a book off the shelf years later, read your notations, and have it all back in your mind.")

In the far corner, sitting behind a desk that was also piled high with books and papers, was the man I often saw charging down the hall or standing before me in class.

"What can I do for you, Michael?"

He knew my name! I later came to realize that he knew virtually everyone's name and could retain each name for years.

I started by asking a question about a paper he had assigned in class. It was only camouflage, however. I was still uneasy about asking for a block of his precious time.

He answered my question thoughtfully and then asked, "Anything else?"

"Would it be possible, I mean, could you give me perhaps a block of time? . . . If you're too busy, I understand."

Without looking up he opened his briefcase and dug around for his Day-Timer. "How about Wednesday at 2:00?"

I had no idea whether or not I was free at that exact time, but I was determined that, no matter what, I would be free. "That would be great!"

I turned and walked out of his office, closing the door with the characteristic rattle of the frosted glass pane. Though I could not have put it into words then, I was a different person from the one who had walked into that office ten minutes earlier. I had been taken seriously by a person for whom I had the highest regard. If he thought I was worthy of an hour of his time every week, then just maybe I was worth something.

It's just the same in our walk with Jesus. Once we realize how intensely He desires to spend time with us, how could we ever see ourselves as worthless again? That moment, Bill, perhaps without knowing it, was really teaching me about the Lord—only the first of many "lived-out" *lessons. Jesus did not come primarily to give us truths. He came to give us Himself. Bill sat there in that cluttered office, not primarily to reproduce more scholars like himself. He was there to offer the greatest gift anyone can give. He was there to give himself.*

"I am a man under authority."

    I had to get special permission to take Bill's *Life of Paul* class, since it was a graduate class and I was still an undergraduate. I tried first to get into his New Testament 100 class, but it was already full. Had I known what I was getting myself into, I would have put off studying under Dr. Lane for a year or two, but one of the great graces of God is that we rarely know what we are really getting ourselves into.

On the first day, he strode into class, armed with his syllabi. He stood before the class, looking us over, seeing if we were ready to hear what he was about to say.

"I am William Lane," he said with a seriousness that made me uncomfortable. "And all you need to know about me is, I am a man under authority—the authority of God's Word, the authority of the Lordship of Jesus Christ!"

At the outset he wanted us to know that even though we would be under his considerable authority for the semester, he, too, was a man under authority. This knowledge marvelously leveled the professor and his students without undermining him in the least.

From that moment, though I barely knew him, I experienced something unique about our relationship. My ears seemed to be tuned to his voice. I am, even today, able to recall practically everything he ever said to me. It was as if God had designed my ears to receive this man's wisdom.

Bill loved to use the example of two tuning forks. "If you take two C tuning forks, tap one and simply hold it next to the other, the one that wasn't tapped will begin to resonate. It's like that with hearts as well," he would say. "Sometimes when we hear God's Word, something inside our hearts starts to resonate. That is because we were created to hear His Word."

Bill lectured with an infectious enthusiasm, often pacing between the rows of seats. Occasionally he would embellish a lecture with a booming hymn that originated more from a Christ-centered childlikeness than from naiveté. His class became the high point of every week. Being prepared was not a priority, but the priority. Making an A wasn't the point; pleasing him was.

～

The middle of the term came before any of us realized it. Bill had not yet given us any papers to write or any tests. In student terms this means that an inordinate amount of weight would be accorded to only a couple of exams. In a class like the Life of Paul, that was a pretty scary prospect!

Finally, close to midterm, Bill announced that a test would be given at the end of the week. He would be out of town at a professional meeting, so a graduate student would proctor the exam. Bill would return on the next Monday. We would "be responsible" for all the material up to this point. He might as well have said, "You will be having your heads chopped off on Friday."

We all crammed as best we could in our desperate little study groups, going over reams of class notes. To emphasize the importance of the exam, I seem to remember we were even given the day before off to prepare. That Friday we came together, not unlike our forefathers gathering in the bowels of the Roman arenas, waiting to be thrown to the lions.

In reality, it was worse than we had imagined. None of us had ever seen a test like this. Pages and pages of questions asking for lengthy interaction on the smallest and most obscure points. Not a fill-in-the-blank or multiple-choice question to be seen anywhere! The exam called for Ph.D.-level responses. I remember staggering out of the room somewhat dizzy and wondering if it was too late to drop the course without getting an "incomplete."

Bill returned on Monday, as he said he would. The graduate student who met his plane was reported to have said, "Your Life of Paul students are dropping the class like flies!"

The next time class met, there were already several empty seats. I only came back in order to ask him in person about dropping the class. Bill didn't seem fazed at all as he walked in with the pile of graded test papers under his arm. He proceeded to hand them out in silence, walking up and down the aisle placing the papers facedown on the proper desks. He did not have to call out each individual; he already knew all our names.

I didn't even look up at him when he came to my desk. I turned the paper over; "43" was written in red at the top! I tried not to let my face show my emotions, lest one of my classmates might be looking at me. I'm dead, I thought.

When Bill was done passing the papers out, he sat down casually on his desk at the front of the classroom. The expression on his face indicated that he was about to say something important. My guess was that it would be one of his favorite phrases, "Lo rachamim." Hebrew for "No mercy!" I can still taste the fear in my mouth at the sound of his mischievous words.

After a long pause, he began. "I want you all to know how disappointed I am in you."

I thought, This is going to be worse than I imagined.

"I want you all to know that I am disappointed in you because you did not trust me." The tone of his voice sounded hurt. "*You should have known that I would adjust the grades, given the low scores.*"

I had heard Bill speak from his intellect for some six grueling weeks. This was the first time I remember ever hearing him speak from the heart. In his characteristic naiveté, he could not understand why so many others had already dropped out without even speaking to him.

"It is more important to say 'I trust you' than it is to say 'I love you,'" Bill often said. We had not trusted him and he was disappointed. Moreover, he was hurt.

Bill was the professor; we were the students. He had the rightful authority to ruin us with those test grades—we had failed, and miserably so. But Bill was a man under authority of a different kind. He had learned that this kind of authority cares for its own and can always be trusted to give a compassionate response.

That was when I decided I would take every class he offered. I ended up doing that; in six years I missed only one of his classes—one on the Dead Sea Scrolls. I realized that I wanted to study with Bill, despite the effect it would have on my grade average. A hard-won C from him meant more than an A from almost anyone else.

The Cycle of Discipleship

⌒ WHENEVER WE ARE faced with a challenge, like mentoring another person, we must learn to "flee to the life of Jesus." In any given situation, we should always ask the question, "What would Jesus do?" or "How did Jesus accomplish this?" In order to do this, we must all become experts on His life.

The life of Christ is the only perfect life we have. In the Gospels we see a series of perfect encounters, of perfect lessons and sayings. Whatever Jesus said or did—or didn't say or do—was the perfect response.

Whatever Jesus said to Nicodemus was the perfect words to have said or to have not said, at that moment, about that subject. Whatever He said to the woman at the well or to the Sadducees or to the Pharisees or to His disciples was perfect. Because of their perfection we will never be able to probe them deeply enough or simply squeeze them dry.

Bill Lane knew this, and that's why he approached the topic of discipleship from the foundational question, "How did Jesus disciple?" In the Gospels we find a simple but deliberate pattern that Jesus used to nurture and encourage, to train and prepare His disciples.

During our last months together, Bill taught a Bible study on what he referred to as "the cycle of discipleship." Though he was beginning to experience some of the final stages of myeloma, he faithfully taught the class. Most of us realized that this would be his final lesson.

Bill saw three phases in Jesus' pattern of discipleship. The first we find in Mark 3:13–15; it is *the call to be with Jesus.* The second phase, which is in Mark 6:7, 12–13, represents *the commissioning of the disciples.* The third is in Mark 6:30–31; here we see the disciples *returning to Jesus,* reporting to Him all the things they had seen and heard. At this moment they heard the word from Jesus, "Come away with me by yourselves to a quiet place and get some rest." Bill used this cycle in his relationships with the students he mentored, as well as in his own walk with the Lord.

PART II

The Call

Called to Conflict

JESUS NEVER CLAIMED that our lives as His disciples would be easy. In fact, one of the realities of encountering Jesus is that when people are truly faced with His being, His truth, they inevitably stumble. He strikes a chord in people's hearts, and sometimes it is a discordant one. His perfect life exposes all that is imperfect in us, and conflict inevitably results.

After Jesus called His disciples, He called them to be *with Him* as He faced several different conflicts. These situations formed a focused time of preparation for the moment when He would send them out to speak His Word and do His work. Some of these conflicts were common to all human beings; some were the kind of conflicts that come only as a direct result of allegiance to Jesus.

Conflict with Family, Religious Leaders, and Hometown Folk

The first situation is found in Mark 3:20–35:

Then Jesus entered a house, and again a crowd gathered, so that he and his disciples were not even able to eat. When his family heard about this, they went to take charge of him, for they said, "He is out of His mind." (3:20–21)

Here we see Jesus in conflict with His own family. You seldom hear sermons on this text. Jesus' mother and brothers went looking for Him. When they finally found Him, He was inaccessible, in a house crammed full of people. Someone sent word to Jesus saying, "Your mother and brothers are outside looking for you." Jesus responded, "Who are my mother and my brothers? . . . Whoever does God's will is my brother and sister and mother."

To some this sounds like a harsh, unfeeling response from Jesus, but we forget that Mary and the brothers had come to take Jesus away. They were convinced, Mark tells us, He was "out of His mind." The ministry had become such a pressing concern that Jesus and His disciples hadn't even taken the time to eat.

In verse 22 and following, we see Jesus and His disciples in yet another situation of conflict. This time it was with the biblical scholars who had come from Jerusalem. They decided that He was demon-possessed. Again, it is important to realize that Jesus purposely has the disciples "with Him." Jesus knows that later, when He sends them out, the disciples will experience this same conflict with religious leaders and it makes an enormous difference whether they face conflict on their own or they face it with Jesus.

The next situation of conflict into which Jesus called His disciples is in Mark 6:1–6:

> Jesus left there and went to his home town, accompanied by his disciples. When the Sabbath came, he began to teach in the synagogue, and many who heard him were amazed.
>
> "Where did this man get these things?" they asked. "What's this wisdom that has been given him, that he even does miracles! Isn't this the carpenter? Isn't this Mary's son and the brother of James, Joses, Judas and Simon? Aren't his sisters here with us?" And they took offense at him.
>
> Jesus said to them, "Only in his home town, among his relatives and in his own house is a prophet without honor." He could not do any miracles there, except lay

his hands on a few sick people and heal them. And he was amazed at their lack of faith.

When Jesus taught in the synagogue in His hometown, the townspeople were struck by His teaching style, which was totally different from anything they were used to. They were used to hearing the rabbis, who taught by quoting other rabbis. (Even today in rabbinic seminaries, if you are a brilliant rabbinic scholar, your brilliance is based on how many other rabbis you are able quote on any one issue.) Jesus' teaching was radically different, and the people were offended by its freshness. They were especially scandalized, it seems, by His humble origins. He was one of them! And yet He was so completely "other."

And so, Jesus found it difficult to carry out His ministry of the Word and healing there in His own hometown. Mark tells us that in this incident, it was Jesus who was amazed by their lack of faith.

Why did Jesus allow the disciples to participate in these experiences of conflict? And why did Bill Lane include these particular incidents in his description of the call of discipleship? Jesus wanted His disciples to be *with Him* in the face of personal rejection. He knew that the call of God on the disciples' lives meant that they would also find themselves in conflict with their own families and with biblical scholars (and practically everyone else).

Learning to deal with rejection is an important part of preparing for ministry. It seems to be inevitable.

Look at the examples Mark gave us. Who rejected Jesus? The people we would expect? Sinners? No. Instead, it was His own family, biblical scholars, those from His own hometown. When any of us answers the call to ministry, these are the people we least expect to resist us. Yet it is precisely this kind of rejection we most often experience when we go out to speak the Lord's Word and do His work.

Bill's experience resonated with Jesus' words. His own call to ministry had led him at one point into conflict with his family. Many religious leaders looked skeptically at his belief in the authority and integrity of Scripture.

As Bill finished describing these incidents of Jesus' rejection, his voice would raise in timbre and volume as he repeated at the conclusion of each section, "It makes an *e-e-enormous* amount of difference if you face conflict in your own strength—or if you face it *with Jesus.*" That was the message he wanted us all to hear and remember.

Conflict with the Demonic

Mark records two incidents of conflict with the demonic in chapters 4 and 5 (4:35–5:20). The first one, where Jesus was in the storm at sea, is not always looked upon as a demonic event:

That day when evening came, he said to his disciples, "Let us go over to the other side." Leaving the crowd behind, they took him along, just as he was, in the boat. There were also other boats with him. A furious squall came up, and the waves broke over the boat, so that it was nearly swamped. Jesus was in the stern, sleeping on a cushion. The disciples woke him and said to him, "Teacher, don't you care if we drown?"

He got up, rebuked the wind and said to the waves, "Quiet! Be still!" Then the wind died down and it was completely calm. (4:35–39)

Jesus told the storm literally to "be muzzled," an order He consistently addressed to the demon-possessed (see Mark 1:25, for instance). Mark wants us to understand that this was, in fact, an encounter with the demonic. It was an attempt by Satan to wipe out Jesus' ministry virtually before it began. When the storm first arose, the disciples rudely spoke to Jesus. "Don't you care if we drown?" they asked. Once the storm subsided, they were amazed—and terrified. And they asked, "Who is this?"

It is important that Mark placed the story of the storm here, because it prepares us to hear about Jesus' dealing directly with a demon-possessed man in chapter 5. First Jesus calmed the sea, then He calmed the demon-possessed man.

Here was a man who had lived in the tombs and had all

the classic symptoms of demonic possession. The center of his personality had been taken over by several demons; in fact, when asked, the demon gave his name as "Legion." He cut himself with stones and no one could subdue him, both further signs of possession. But Jesus cast out the demon.

In response the man begged to go with Jesus. It is important to note, however, that Jesus would not allow him to become an apostle. We know as well that he was a Gentile; that also explains why it was necessary that Jesus refuse his request. But the key reason was because he had not been *with* Jesus. So the man was sent back to his own family.

That used to bother me. I thought, *What a great drawing card this guy would have been for Jesus' ministry.* But that's not what Jesus was interested in. At that moment Jesus was focusing on investing Himself in the Twelve, and the newly restored man just couldn't be a part of that now. Many are called, Jesus said, but few are chosen. Even though this man would become a witness in his own hometown, Jesus had not called him to be an apostle.

Jesus purposefully brought His disciples into these two situations where they experienced conflict with the demonic, because he knew that as they went out to do His work they would be confronted with demonic powers.

Bill felt it was important to mention these incidents as part of his teaching on discipleship even though few of us, he said, will confront the demonic in such a drastic and direct way. These kinds of manifestations tend to occur most often in Third World countries, though they are certainly not unknown in the U.S. Yet all of us in America face the deterioration of our culture, which is still a direct impact of demonic activity. And Bill wanted us all to know that only Jesus has the power to say, "Be muzzled" to these demonic forces. The people had tried everything to control the demon-possessed man. They had chained him. They had cast him out. But nothing could control him, much less heal him.

Bill would repeat, "It makes an *e-e-enormous* amount of difference if you face conflict in your own strength—or if you face it *with Jesus*." That was the message he wanted us all to hear and remember.

Conflict with Disease and Death

In the final situation we see Jesus in conflict with disease and death (Mark 5:21–43):

When Jesus had again crossed over by boat to the other side of the lake, a large crowd gathered around him. While he was by the lake, one of the synagogue rulers, named Jairus, came there. Seeing Jesus, he fell at his feet and pleaded earnestly with him, "My little daughter is dying. Please come and put your hands on her so that she will be healed and live." So Jesus went with him.

A large crowd followed and pressed around him. And a woman was there who had been subject to bleeding for twelve years. She had suffered a great deal under the care of many doctors and had spent all she had, yet instead of getting better she grew worse. When she heard about Jesus, she came up behind him in the crowd and touched his cloak, because she thought, "If I just touch his clothes, I will be healed." Immediately her bleeding stopped and she felt in her body that she was freed from her suffering.

At once Jesus realized that power had gone out from him. He turned around in the crowd and asked, "Who touched my clothes?"

"You see the people crowding against you," his disciples answered, "and yet you can ask, 'Who touched me?'"

But Jesus kept looking around to see who had done it. Then the woman, knowing what had happened to her, came and fell at his feet and, trembling with fear, told him the whole truth. He said to her, "Daughter, your faith has healed you. Go in peace and be freed from your suffering."

While Jesus was still speaking, some men came from the house of Jairus, the synagogue ruler. "Your daughter is dead," they said. "Why bother the teacher any more?"

Ignoring what they said, Jesus told the synagogue ruler, "Don't be afraid; just believe."

MICHAEL CARD   ～   39

He did not let anyone follow him except Peter, James and John the brother of James. When they came to the home of the synagogue ruler, Jesus saw a commotion, with people crying and wailing loudly. He went in and said to them, "Why all this commotion and wailing? The child is not dead but asleep." But they laughed at him.

After he put them all out, he took the child's father and mother and the disciples who were with him, and went in where the child was. He took her by the hand and said to her, "*Talitha koum!*" (which means, "Little girl, I say to you, get up!"). Immediately the girl stood up and walked around (she was twelve years old). At this they were completely astonished. He gave strict orders not to let anyone know about this, and told them to give her something to eat.

Notice that Jesus called Peter, James, and John to come into the room to be *with Him* when He laid His hands on the little girl. It was important that they be *with Jesus* to witness the power that He has over disease, for they would soon be sent out to do His work.

Likewise, with the woman who apparently was suffering from endometriosis, Mark makes sure that we know that Jesus' disciples are with Him. They, however, are clueless as to what is going on around them. They rudely respond to Jesus' inquiry. But the woman, whose name we will never know, understands in her heart that Jesus alone has the power, even in the hem of His coat, to heal her. There was more healing power in the hem of His garment than in a whole drugstore!

And so the little girl and the grown-up woman become prime examples of Jesus' power over disease and death. Insofar as we also trust and believe in Him, we can hear His words as well, "Don't be afraid; just believe."

If Bill were reciting these events to you, he would again reiterate, "It makes an *e-e-enormous* amount of difference if you face disease and death in your own strength—or if you face it *with Jesus*." Even as he spoke these words for the last time, he was himself engaged in a battle with both of these enemies. He did not face them in his own strength; he faced them *with Jesus*.

So the disciples were *with Jesus* in the context of conflict with His family, the teachers of the law, and his hometown folk; they were with Jesus as He confronted the demonic in the stilling of the storm and also with the man of the tombs; and they were with Jesus in the conflict with disease and death. He wanted to invest in them a wealth of experience *with Him* so that they would be prepared when they were confronted with these experiences. Those of us who have sensed the call of Jesus in our lives would do well to understand that a vital part of that call is a time of intense preparation, a time of being *with Jesus*.

Called to Genuine Relationship

MY RELATIONSHIP WITH Bill didn't last for twenty-five years because I was so much fun to be with, or because I had some special maturity that made him want to spend time with me. In actuality, when we began our walks, I was amazingly immature in almost every way. Nevertheless, Bill hung in there with me as I grew—willing to experience the growing pains with me. In rare moments he let me share in some of his growing pains too.

Being a "soul-friend," as Bill called it, is the only way to experience genuine relationship. It expects so much more of us than a superficial relationship demands. A soul-friend is one who first and foremost loves in a way that desires the best for the other person. This kind of love then demands that we play a part in our friend's journey to grow into the best that Christ has for him. The demands on us may include loving confrontation on one end, ready forgiveness on the other, and vast amounts of patience in between.

As always, Jesus is the greatest example of this. He is always available, always listening, always ready to forgive, yet He feels the pain of rejection. Jesus loved us so deeply that He was willing to go to the cross for us to make possible our relationship with Him. He considered it a joy to endure the pain that was required in order that we might walk as friends. There could be no greater "soul-friend" than the One who first saved our souls!

*"We must be open to becoming
a soul-friend."*

~ *As far as I know it was the only time I ever hurt him.
We were both still at Western. Bill invited me to have breakfast with him early one Monday morning at a local restau-
rant, which was a break from the norm. We often shared
lunch or supper together, but rarely breakfast. And when we
did have "meal fellowship," as he enjoyed calling it, it was
usually shared with others.*

*For some time he had been counseling me through yet
another rough relationship I was in the midst of "breaking
off." That morning he was quieter than usual, which told
me something was up.*

*When we finally settled into a corner booth and ordered
our breakfast, he looked at me and said, "I'm worried about
you, Michael. This is perhaps the third young woman you
have dated since we've known each other, and now you're*

breaking up again. I'm concerned about your ability to sustain a relationship."

He knew better than anyone else just how immature I was, which probably explained his reluctance to bring the matter up in the first place, but he was willing to risk it for my good. Love is always willing to take this kind of risk.

But I was hurt by what sounded to me like criticism. How could he know what I felt? What was he insinuating? At this point in my life I lacked the maturity to receive this kind of love.

"How can you say that to me!" I snapped back. "After all, you are divorced. At least I never did that!"

Bill grew quiet. He had risked genuinely loving me, and, like so many others, I had hurt him for it. "I worked at that relationship as hard as I could for as long as I could," he said, almost in tears. And there the discussion ended.

Anyone else would have decided at this point that walking with someone like me was not worth the trouble. Not Bill. As best I remember, he never brought up the subject again.

A few months before his death, I recalled the incident and asked his forgiveness. It was obvious from his response that he had forgiven me long ago, although I could tell he still remembered the sting of it. All that remained, he said, was for me to forgive myself.

He was trying to instruct me about what it means to be

a soul-friend, which is far more than simply entering into another person's suffering. A true soul-friend is willing to endure the inevitable pain that is caused by being in a relationship with another human being. "We are fragile and fallen people," Bill would say. "Often we hurt each other."

In a genuine relationship, friends always love and always forgive. A true soul-friend understands this and learns to rely totally on God's grace to make it possible.

"The best way to show someone that you love them is to listen to them."

⁓ *"Our age is a dialogue of the deaf," Bill often said. "You must develop a lifestyle of listening," he would say when we were talking about some difficulty I was having with some person or another. Twenty-five years later I have only begun to understand the wisdom of those words.*

"The best way to show someone that you love them is to listen to them," my dear friend told me once on an unforgettable walk we took around the campus. I was agonizing over my future wife, Susan, who at that point was giving me little or no reason for hoping that my affections would ever be returned. Out of my own impatience, I was preparing for a "showdown" with her, a confrontation that would have surely destroyed the fragile relationship we had. I would talk and talk and talk—and she would listen, I hoped, and agree.

"*If you really want to show her you love her,*" Bill said with his characteristic intensity, "*listen to her.*"

He reminded me how frequently Jesus gave this advice. In Luke's Gospel, for instance, Jesus said, "Consider carefully how you listen." And He was forever saying, "He who has ears, let him hear."

At the end of our walk that day Bill had convinced me. I sought from that point on to begin a lifestyle of listening, first listening to Susan and then to our children, Katie, Will, Nathan, and Maggie. Over the years I have discovered again and again the depth of the truth of Bill's words and have sought to share them with as many people as I could. As I seek to listen to the ones I care the most about, they consistently say they feel well loved in the process. And in return I come to know them in ways I could only have dreamed about otherwise. It sometimes approaches an almost mystical feeling when I find myself listening to another William, my eldest son, Bill's namesake.

A Lifestyle of Listening

WHENEVER AN AWESTRUCK student would ask Dr. Lane how he approached Scripture, he would answer, "I *listen* to the text." His consistent prayer was that God would allow him to hear the Word and be made wise by the wisdom of God.

Bill repeated a few phrases again and again. They were his special discoveries, made over a lifetime of listening to his own life, and he repeated them endlessly, it seemed to me. "Timing is of the Lord," was his response, among many others, to my agonized questions about whom I would marry and when.

"Let it simmer on the back burner of your mind," he would say when we would talk about some prospective topic for a paper. I found, indeed, that his advice was true. When I was perplexed by some exegetical problem, I would often go to sleep with it "simmering," only to wake with the solution.

An idea from one of his phrases is still simmering on the back burner of my mind. "You must ask God for a listening heart," he would often say when we would speak about some difficulty I was having with some person or situation. We must listen to the Word, to the silence of prayer, and to the poem of our own lives, for in all these God is speaking. And if God is speaking, then nothing else matters but listening.

Listening to the Word

When it comes to listening to God speak, we must always begin with the Word of God, His clearest and most authoritative voice. But, as in all listening, we must learn to allow the other Person to speak. This may sound oversimplified, but in fact it can be a major task. When we find ourselves trying to listen to someone whose speech is slow or deliberate, the great temptation is to finish their sentences for them. The same is often the case when we listen to God's Word, particularly to familiar passages. Adopting a listening stance before the Word means keeping your mind as quiet as possible and letting the Bible finish its own sentences and stories. Allowing the Bible to speak for itself means listening with as few presuppositions as possible.

Often we fail in listening when we read only for theological or doctrinal affirmation. The baptism of Jesus becomes a proof text for immersion and not a scene to which we are transported by our imagination. The crucifixion becomes a necessary piece of the puzzle for redemption, the obligatory final step in a long *heilsgeschechte* ("holy history"), and not a heartbreaking moment of transformation. Parables and visions become codes to break, sponges to squeeze dry and then leave behind. Sometimes my own temptation is to merely use the Bible as fodder for lyrics.

In all these ways and more, we effectively plug our ears to the Voice of Scripture. The simple act (which is sometimes not so simple) of quieting our minds and hearts and allowing the Bible to speak, as if it has never before spoken in its own voice to you, will transform your time with the Word. Be quiet, be patient, and *let Scripture say what it has to say!*

Bill loved to remind us that in the ancient world all reading was done out loud. "This is how everyone was taught to read," he would say. Even when one was alone, reading was done audibly. That is how Philip knew from what section of the Old Testament the Ethiopian eunuch was reading in Acts 8. He came upon the eunuch sitting on his chariot, reading from the book of the prophet Isaiah aloud to himself.

Keep in mind that the Scriptures were read from the beginning in this way and were no doubt written with this in mind. So try reading them out loud to yourself. There is no way to estimate the impact of hearing the sound of your own voice speak the words of Scripture.

Listening to the Silence of Prayer

Prayer teaches us that we must learn to listen not only to words, but also to the silence, for, as Mother Teresa said, "God speaks in the silence of the heart."

While I was at Western I attended a seminar with Bill in which Eberhard Bethge, the great friend and biographer of Dietrich Bonhoeffer, shared a story of their days in the underground seminary (Hitler had closed all the seminaries). When the young men whom Bonhoeffer was discipling in their clandestine seminary complained to him that their minds were wandering during their mandatory two-hour-long silent prayer sessions, he told them not to fight the distractions.

"Follow your mind wherever it goes," Bonhoeffer said. "Follow your thoughts until they stop, and then wherever they stop, make that person or problem a matter for prayer. Fighting it may only lead to more noise and inner turmoil."

We must learn to allow the Other to speak in prayer. We all have friends who dominate the conversation. Are we that sort of friend to God? Who has the more worthwhile things to say?

As in Bible reading, sometimes it is helpful to break old habits. If your prayers seem long, simply pray the

Lord's Prayer. The simplicity of it will be refreshing, and more time will be left for listening. Remember Jesus gave this prayer in response to the request, "Lord, teach us to pray."

Our physical attitude during prayer is also important. Some find it best to kneel. I've heard it said that the discomfort from kneeling on a hard floor helps some people to focus. (Bill preferred to sit comfortably upright in a chair.) Jesus' brother James was said to have knees like a camel from all the time he spent in prayer. Some sit upright, some walk, some drive, some lie facedown. The focus is not the posture or some gimmick; the focus is solely upon the Voice of the One who speaks in the silence of the heart, and we must become quiet, faithful, and courteous listeners.

God speaks through the words of Scripture, through the silence of prayer, and also through the poem of our lives.

Listening to the Poem of Our Lives

Your life is a poem, a song, a parable. In essence, Paul told the Ephesians, "We are God's masterpieces, poems . . ." (2:10). The Bible gives abundant examples of lives that were living parables:

- Abraham offered his son to God, a parable of God's offering His own Son for us. (Gen. 22:1–18)

- Jacob wrestled with God, a parable of the struggle we all have in finding faith. (Gen. 32:22–31)

- Job suffered enormous losses, a parable of discovering the truth that God doesn't always give us answers, but He always gives us Himself. (Job 1–42)

The best way to learn to listen to the parable of your life is to examine the parables of Jesus and learn how to listen to them.

Bill believed that the parable is not simply one form of communication among many. He taught us that it is *the* paradigm for communication. It is an extended metaphor that, through extension, has come to life with characters and a story. A metaphor simply says, "This is like that."

But a parable is able to enlarge the statement; this is how this is like that, this is what that means or can mean, this is what this means for you. The extension of the metaphor into parable allows you and me to become characters in the story, since we tend to identify with one or another character in the parable. You are the boy who strayed off with the family riches. I am the older jealous son whose teeth were set on edge by the return of the prodigal. Perhaps you are the woman who was on her hands and knees all day, searching for the treasure of a single lost coin. The parable draws us in, forces us to participate or get out altogether. It is just the same with our lives.

Like the parables of Jesus, our lives often lack closure. By this I do not mean that they don't have endings in and of themselves. The boy returns home, the judge finally listens to the widow, the pearl is found. But what is often left silent in Jesus' parables is the moral, the summation, and the conclusion. Within the freedom of the form of the parable, Jesus leaves the "aha!" to us. The moment of realization is ours to savor. That is the parable's greatest strength as well as its greatest weakness. The transcendent moment when the eyes of the heart are opened is left for you to experience alone with the Spirit.

Like parables, our lives also often lack closure. But this should not be seen as a frustration; rather, it should be understood as an invitation to listen! For it is still Jesus who is creating the story as you live day by day. Like the parable, you are allowed not only to be one character in the story; more important, you are invited to identify with the other characters in the parable that is your life. And through identification with others, you experience to the fullest all that your parable means. The moral, the explanation, is left to us to discover by listening to Scripture and prayer.

We must develop a lifestyle of listening. All around and through and especially in us, God speaks. If God is speaking, then nothing else matters but listening!

Called to Be with Christ

THOUGH I FIRST sensed the call of God on my life when I was eight years old, it was not until I began to walk with Bill that my calling began to take shape. Moreover, in the years that followed, Bill would help to train and equip me to fulfill that calling. No disciple could ever hope for more. He would always direct me to the life of Jesus whenever I was struggling. He taught me that within that perfect life I would always find whatever I needed.

The call of Jesus is, at its most basic, a call to simply be *with Him*. Have you noticed how many times in the Gospels Jesus simply said, "Follow Me"? He says, "Follow Me," and our sacred privilege is to respond.

The disciples learned volumes by being *with Him* as He faced rejection, by being *with Him* as He went head-on against demons, by being *with Him* as he conquered disease and death.

We, too, are called to watch Him walk, talk, teach, heal, rebuke, rest, die—to listen to His life. For our part, we must take the time to let Him be who He is while we remain still, listening, watching, learning.

In that companionship, we learn truly who Jesus really is, the content of His character and the shape of His life. This is essential before we can be commissioned, before we can do His work and speak His word.

It was an unusually quiet walk for us. Most often we chattered away, but perhaps because of the muffling effect of the snow or the deserted campus, or maybe because we were beginning to understand how precious is the silence that precedes speech, we slogged through the knee-deep snow without a word.

"You seem quiet," I finally said. This, too, was a break from the norm, since it was Bill who always plied me with questions.

"Really? I'm just enjoying the time," he said. "Would it be all right if we just walked quietly today?"

This was a new dimension for me. Dr. Lane, not as an answer man or counselor, not as a discussion partner, but as a companion. He did not seem to feel the need to fill up the time with talk, and by doing so he added a precious value to our time together. It was not that he was distracted by some other issue. He was not lost in thought. He was "mindful" that afternoon and invited me into that intensely personal space with him, a space that needs no words, only presence.

Once again Jesus was using Bill to teach me about Himself. This is the kind of time He desires with us. Not busy but slow time. Time not necessarily filled with words, but always with His presence. For those of us who need it, what could possibly be more affirming than to be invited to take a walk with Jesus, not because of our intellect, or our ability to ask or answer questions, not because we are pretty or fun to be with, but simply because He desires to be with us? He wants to fill our empty, silent lives with the fullness of His presence.

Sonship Is Established in the Wilderness

⁓ OUR FAVORITE BIBLICAL themes invariably overlap our personal themes, and so one of the themes to which Bill returned again and again was the theme of the wilderness, the *eremos topos* in Greek. It was one of the organizing motifs in his commentary on the book of Mark. It was one of the central categories he used in understanding the heart and mind of Jesus. And it was also a window through which he viewed the fallen world. I believe it helped him make some sense out of the senselessness of it all. There was a purpose in the suffering; there had to be.

Bill's motto: "Sonship/daughterhood is established in the wilderness."(Even in the early seventies he used inclusive language.) As with his other seemingly simple sayings, a wealth of biblical material was behind each word.

God had called Israel into the wilderness so that they

could learn how much they needed Him. He provided water from the rock. He fed them manna. Their shoes never wore out. When they were threatened, God would simply say, "Stand still and I will fight for you." In the wilderness Israel learned how much they needed God. They learned there that they were helpless and hopeless without Him. At the end of that learning time, God announced through the prophet Hosea, "Out of Egypt I called my son" (Hosea 11:1).

"So," Bill would announce just as prophetically, "the sonship of Israel was established in the wilderness." In the wilderness Israel learned that they had a Father, after all.

The same is true in the life of Jesus, because if anything is ultimately true, you'll find it reflected in His perfect life. Mark 1:4 tells us that John was baptizing repentant Jews in the wilderness when Jesus arrived on the crowded scene (John's peculiar, previously unheard of form of baptism was for repentance; before that, the Jews had only practiced proselyte baptism).

On the first day, Jesus was merely standing in the crowd among the Pharisees when the Baptist announced, "Among you stands one you do not know" (John 1:26). The next day, as Jesus returned to the river, John looked up and saw Him once more. "Look, the Lamb of God!" he shouted to everyone. And then the inexplicable happened. Jesus asked John to baptize *Him.*

But what could Jesus, the spotless Lamb, possibly have to repent of? And so John protested because he did not, perhaps could not, understand Jesus' request. He understood that it should be Jesus who should baptize him.

Jesus was insistent. John humbly obeyed. At that moment the Sonship of Jesus was proclaimed by a voice from heaven: "You are my Son, whom I love; with you I am well pleased" (Mark 1:11).

At once, Mark tells us, the Holy Spirit who had descended on Jesus like a dove at His baptism drove Jesus into the wilderness, of all places. His Sonship, announced by the voice of His Father, would now be demonstrated and established in the wilderness. Here Jesus experienced an intensified period of temptation, not for forty years but forty days. Here Jesus demonstrated that He already knew what it took Israel eighty years to learn (if indeed they ever learned it): He was totally dependent on the Father and the Father's Word. Throughout the Gospel of John, Jesus insisted again and again, "I can do nothing without the Father."

When the issue of bread came up once more and the devil, in essence, wanted Jesus to provide manna for Himself, Jesus responded in a way that any young believer might respond: He simply quoted the Bible. It is not bread that sustains, Jesus said, but the Word of God. Every time Satan tempted Him, Jesus responded with the

Word. Finally the devil left Him "for a time." Then, thankfully, Matthew lets us know that angels ministered to Jesus.

The Sonship of Jesus, like Israel's sonship, was demonstrated and established in the wilderness.

The application? Our sonship, our daughterhood, is also established in the wilderness. There are times when, like the dove, God's Spirit drives us to a barren place where we must learn to totally depend on Him and upon His Word.

If you are reading this from a wilderness place, I want to encourage you to focus on a couple of truths. First, realize that you cannot get out of the wilderness on your own. This is not a pull-yourself-up-by-your-spiritual-bootstraps affair. Instead, I encourage you to wait for God to find you. Trust His sufficiency. After all, He is the Good Shepherd. He will leave ninety-nine perfectly good sheep to find you and me.

Second, don't stop reading your Bible or praying, even though it all seems as dry as dust. After all, it is always dry in the desert. If you can only manage one word of Scripture, that's enough. If you can only utter one word in prayer, then let it be the name *Jesus*, for even His name is a prayer.

Time after time when I would come to Bill with some problem or some ordeal I was going through, he would look at me as if he understood that more was going on than the often petty, superficial circumstances. By the wilderness experience God was establishing me as His son. Bill understood this from Scripture and from his own experience, and thankfully, he passed it on.

In the Wilderness

~~~ Sometimes a true mentor is sent to seek us out in the wilderness. I learned this in 1983 when Bill "found" me. I had been burning the candle at both ends for many months, trying to write, perform concerts, and be a new husband all at the same time—and doing a miserable job at all of these. Adding to the pressure was a bitter dispute with the record company at the time.

It all began to fall apart at a concert in Louisville, Kentucky. Looking back on it now, I believe I must have been nearing a nervous breakdown. My wife, Susan, sensing my struggle, called Bill to ask for prayer. He was still in Bowling Green at the university, a couple of hours away. After hearing what was going on, he dropped whatever he was doing and drove to Louisville. He didn't tell me he was coming.

As the time for the concert drew near, I was seriously beginning to wonder if I would be able to get up and minister to anyone at all, given the shape I was in. Just then, out of nowhere, Bill walked in. I remember him carrying his coat draped over his arm; I suppose he had not taken the time to put it on after he got out of the car. He was in a hurry. He was worried about me.

He gave me one of his big bear hugs and we both wept. I thought my problem was brokenness, but as he put his arms around me I felt something deeper breaking, inside my soul, that still needed to be broken. Sonship is established in the wilderness.

God calls each one of us to the wilderness to make us His sons and daughters. In the wilderness we learn how much we need Him. In the wilderness we learn to become totally dependent on His Word. In the wilderness He seeks us out, His miserable lost sheep. And sometimes He sends one of His servants to find us in the wilderness of our weariness and confusion.

PART III

The Commission

Sent to Do His Work

⁓ OFTEN WHEN I was about to set off on a long trip, the phone would ring. It would be Bill reminding me that he would be in prayer for our team each night of the tour. He would commit the itinerary to memory so that he could better pray for us. He would remind me that it was not my work, but Jesus' that I was called to do; they were not to be my words but His.

After the disciples had been called and prepared, they were commissioned to go out and speak Jesus' word and do His work. Mark described this moment (6:7, 12–13):

> Calling the Twelve to him, he sent them out two by two and gave them authority over evil spirits . . .
>
> They went out and preached that people should repent. They drove out many demons and anointed many sick people with oil and healed them.

There is more behind the literal meaning of the Greek word *apostolos* than just "the ones who are sent." Behind the word *apostle* is an ancient Hebrew concept called the *shelliock*, a term indicating someone who was given authority in legal matters. For example, if someone wanted to purchase a piece of land but was unable to be present to close the deal, he would appoint a *shelliock*, giving that person the authority to go in his place. The closest parallel we have to this in our time is an attorney. When my attorney represents me, he speaks with my authority. That is precisely the idea of the apostle. We find this kind of representative language throughout the Gospels:

- *If they obeyed my teaching, they will obey yours also.* (John 15:20)

- *Whatever you did for one of the least of these brothers of mine, you did for me.* (Matt. 25:40)

This idea signifies one-on-one identification. "If they reject you, they are really rejecting me," Jesus said. Why? Because the apostles were acting as His *shelliockim*, as His authoritative representatives. The *shelliock* is one who is sent with Jesus' authority to do His work and to speak His word.

*"Let the excellence of your work
be your protest."*

⁓ *Perhaps I had been away from Bill's influence too
long. Maybe it was merely "world-weariness." But a bitterness in my heart and soul, caused by focusing on what I
believed were the "evils" of the Christian music industry,
had almost incapacitated me. Bill was far away in
Washington at Seattle Pacific University by now, and we
only connected by phone every few weeks. Perhaps once a
year I would go there or he would come to Nashville, and we
would have a chance to walk together. In 1996, on one of his
visits for a biblical society meeting here, he stayed in our
home, delighted to see his "adopted" grandchildren.*

*He had often heard me complain about the Christian
music business. Sometimes he would correct me: "Anything
you say publicly will only sound like sour grapes." Often he
would commiserate, since he had struggled with many of*

the same attitudes in the academic world. But now he was hearing a level of bitterness that he said alarmed him.

It was not spoken as one of his maxims; in fact, I remember it was buried somewhere inside a sentence. We were walking in the woods around my house, going back and forth on the issues of ministry versus business—and how to maintain spiritual integrity.

"Let the excellence of your work be your protest," he said. "Take the energy you're wasting with complaining and bitterness, and focus it on your craft. If you are going to protest the state of the industry, do so by making your work the best it can be."

This did not sound like a new idea for Bill. In his own world of academic politics and publishing, he had fought his version of this battle against a bitter spirit and, for the most part, had won.

Yet this is, of course, a naive notion—to combat shallowness and shoddiness with excellence in a world that rewards the former with fame. But this is the kind of childlike naiveté that made Bill a man of God. He believed that this world is not all there is, that there is One who will reward us based on a radically different value system.

He had gone on before me in this particular battle, and if he had not found absolute victory, he had at least discovered a motto to mutter to himself in the heat of the battle. "Let the excellence of your work be your protest."

Shortly before his death, an Irish friend who was a sign painter from Belfast, lettered these words on the wall of our recording studio in Franklin, Tennessee. Every day as we hammer out melodies and lyrics, these words watch over us, reminding us in their naive way: This is where you can best spend yourselves in the battle.

The Ozette Triangle: Loosing the Sandal Thong

⁓ One of Bill's many areas of interest was Jewish backgrounds. He had studied rabbinics and Judaism, all with an eye to illuminating the New Testament. One fragment he loved to share had to do with a rabbinic mandate regarding the limitations placed on the service a disciple owed to his teacher: "Every task that a slave does for his master will a student do for his teacher except for the loosing of the sandal thong."

For a student to abase himself to take off a rabbi's sandal was seen as too demeaning a task, and so the mandate was given.

Bill applied this piece of background first to John the Baptist saying in Mark 1:7 that he was not worthy to loosen the thong of Jesus' sandal, then to the passage in John 13, where Jesus washed the disciples' feet. His observation was that even though John the Baptist's statement *demonstrated a genuine humility, Jesus' humility exceeded that of John's because He was not only willing to loosen their shoes but even to wash their feet.*

It was February 1994, and Bill was still at S.P.U. From the past several conversations we'd had on the phone, he was able to sense that I was rapidly approaching burnout once again, and he, too, was in a weary place, and so the invitation came to spend a week with him hiking in the wilderness. "We'll hike the Ozette Triangle," he said, his voice almost breaking with excitement.

We could afford only one hotel room with a sitting room and a single bed. As was his custom, he insisted on taking the couch in the other room while I slept in the bed. The mentality of the loosened sandal!

The Ozette Triangle is a unique hike. During the first leg we hiked through virgin forest. During the second side of the triangle we made our way along the shore of the Pacific to a place called Wedding Rock, where all sorts of petroglyphs, carved on the rocks hundreds of years ago by Indians, still remain. As we climbed over the rocks and discovered a carving, we felt as if we were the first to discover it. Some of the petroglyphs were not so ancient since they pictured three-masted ships; but regardless, we were touching another place and another culture from long ago. Like kids we photographed every petroglyph we could find and planned someday to research and catalog them (Bill later sent me some rough drawings as our first step in this process). On the final leg of the hike, we walked through the only temperate rain forest in the United States. If you let your imagination go, you can almost see pterodactyls overhead!

This was Bill in his element, even more than in the classroom. We walked along a beach covered with multicolored stones. "Oooooh, look at this one," he cried. "Beautiful!" With an infectious childlikeness Bill turned over each stone, all the while collecting sand dollars and shells. (We found out later we were on an Indian reservation, which made it illegal for us to collect sand dollars and so, dejected, we brought back our treasures and did our best to scatter them on the beach.)

As we finished the day's hiking and got back to the car, Bill seemed especially exhausted. Perhaps he was experiencing some of the early effects of his myeloma. He settled into the passenger seat of the car and began trying to take off his hiking boots. Whenever he bent over, he got light-headed. After a couple of attempts, he looked at me sheepishly and asked, "Will you help me with my boots?"

With a great amount of effort, he swung his leg over onto my lap, and I unlaced and removed his boots. He handed me his socks and tennis shoes as well to put on for him.

Often the most mystical and transcendent experiences come through the most mundane occurrences. Brother Lawrence, while washing dishes, was struck by the most *sublime vision of how to commune with God. Augustine smelled the flowers in his garden and heard a child's school rhyme, "Take and Read," and sensed God's urging to go and read the Scripture, which changed his life and ultimately the world. You and I help a homeless person and experience the presence of Jesus. We change a dirty diaper and are filled with the feeling of God's parental love for His children. Loosening the laces of Bill's boot that afternoon was just such an experience for me: transcendent. It seemed to be a graduation into a new dimension of discipleship, an initiation into a divine mystery, a sacramental moment for us both.*

"Every task that a slave does for his master will a student do for his teacher except . . ." Jesus showed us that there are no exceptions to loving someone. Therefore, every task will be done by disciple and teacher alike, by master and slave, to and for each other, for the sake of Christ.

The Servant-Lordship of Jesus

⁓ BILL ONCE SAID, "The washing of the disciples' feet was a defining moment of Jesus' ministry." Then he paused for a moment to emphasize his next words. "It is a moment that should define us as well, for we are the ones, as His disciples, who wash the feet of the brothers and sisters with the water of God's Word."

If you look at the text of Philippians 2:6–11, you will see that it is set aside in the margins as a hymn that was sung in the early church. This ancient hymn tells us that Christ came in the form of a servant. Jesus Himself said, "I came to serve, not to be served," and if you look at His life with the disciples, you might sometimes think He was their butler. When they were hungry, He fed them. When they were tired, He took them aside so they could rest.

Three times, in the Garden of Gethsemane, when He

was in agony, sweating blood, *three times* He interrupted His prayer to go check on them to make sure they were not falling into temptation. That is amazing! What could have been more unexpected than a Messiah who washed feet, one who came to serve and not to be served?

The very first song I wrote at Bill's request, "Stranger on the Shore," was based on a sermon he had written on what he was always careful to refer to as the *second* miraculous catch of fish. There were two miraculous catches of fish in the Bible: one early in Jesus' ministry when Peter fell down before Him and said, "Go away from me, Lord; I am a sinful man." That is in the gospel of Luke (5:4–11). The second occurrence is in John 21. (There are also two temple cleansings in the Bible. The first, early in His ministry, practically the first public thing Jesus ever did, is recorded only in John 2:13–17, and the second as almost His last public act, in the Synoptic Gospels [Matt. 21; Mark 11; Luke 19]. A lot of people don't realize this, and Bill loved pointing it out.)

The account in John begins with Peter stating, "I'm going fishing. Who's going with me?" The disciples went out all night and didn't catch anything. As they were coming back in, they saw Someone standing on the shore. But they did not know who He was.

The fact is, no one recognized Jesus after the Resurrection. Mary thought He was the gardener; it wasn't until

He spoke her name that she recognized Him. It is just the same with us. We recognize His voice. But like Mary, we don't always recognize His appearance.

The disciples, on the way to Emmaus, walked and talked with Jesus long enough for Him to explain everything in the Old Testament concerning Himself, which must have taken hours, yet they did not know who He was. They did not recognize Him until He broke the bread. We, too, recognize Him in the breaking of the bread.

Likewise, in John, the disciples did not recognize the One on the shore. Just then Jesus, who specializes in asking irritating questions, asked them the most insulting question you could ask a fisherman: "You haven't caught any fish, have you?" They shouted back, "No (as if it were any of your business), we haven't caught any fish."

Then Jesus called out, "Throw your nets on the starboard side. You'll find some," and they did. John looked down at the net full of fish. He didn't recognize Jesus. But he remembered being present at the first miraculous catch of fish. He looked at the net full of fish and gasped, "It's the Lord!"

Just then Peter did something peculiar, even for him. John remembered the detail that Peter had taken off most of his clothes, because he had been working. Now Peter took the time to put his clothes back on and *then* jumped in the water. Has this detail ever bothered you? Bill always said that details in Scripture are important; they are always there for a reason. The purpose for this strange detail, I believe, is that Peter thought he was going to walk back to the shore, *on the water*. After all, he'd walked on water once before. Why else would he take the time to put his clothes back on and then jump in?

In any case, the disciples pulled the boats up to the shore, close to Jesus, yet they still weren't sure it was Him. John said in chapter 21, verse 12, "None of the disciples dared ask him, 'Who are you?'" They knew it was the Lord, but somehow at the same time, they didn't know it was Him.

The important question is, Why was Jesus there? Was He surrounded by angels, inviting the disciples to fall down on the sand and worship Him? Certainly that would have been appropriate for the risen Lord, the Lord of glory.

Despite the fact that He had endured the Cross for them and stood now before them with scars on His body from what He had suffered, He had come to make them breakfast. He was doing what he always did—the same yesterday, today, and forever, He had come to take care of them as their Servant Lord!

Beside Jesus the apostles saw a fire. The apostle John recorded an important detail: the fire had burned low as Jesus waited for them, as if He'd had nothing better to do.

There were fish cooking on the fire (He could catch fish that day, even if they couldn't). The risen Lord, the Lord of glory, had waited there to make breakfast for them.

This is more than some sterile object lesson. Jesus truly longed to be with them once more. That is why He was there. He knew that they were tired, He knew they'd been out all night long, He knew they couldn't catch any fish. He wanted to take care of them because that's how love expresses itself.

The fact that Jesus was not there with angels, that instead He came simply to make breakfast, makes me want to fall down and worship Him all the more. I don't know much about angels, and I don't know anything about glory, although I am not sure if glory is something I'm naturally drawn to. But I have tasted servanthood, and I know that my heart is warmed and drawn by a Savior-Servant who only desires to wash my feet with the water of His Word.

This very moment Jesus is serving us. He's interceding before the Father for us, right now. He's preparing a place just for us. (For all I know, He's building furniture.) This very moment He wants to wash our feet. He wants you and me to put our dirty feet, our dirty lives, into His hands so that He can make them clean. We do not really understand who He is until we see that He is delighted to do just that.

"I want to show you how a Christian man dies."

~ It is the fall of 1995. I am in the back of a tour bus, parked beside an auditorium on the campus of Gordon College. Bill had taught at the divinity school across the street in the late '60s. Being here always makes me think of him.

By now he is in Seattle, dean of the School of Religion at Seattle Pacific University, so I call to see how he is doing.

His voice is uncharacteristically grave. "I have some bad news," he said. "Brenda and I just got back some blood tests. The doctor says it looks like multiple myeloma. It's cancer."

I don't know what to say. How should I respond to this man who means more to me than I could ever put into words?

Then, sensing my feelings from two thousand miles away, Bill says something extraordinary for a person who could be facing death. His words are soft. "Michael, don't be afraid."

But I am afraid, so afraid I am practically blinded to what he might be experiencing just now. Deeper down in a more selfish place, I am afraid of what my world will be like without him in it. He goes on to give me the sketchy details as he understands them. (He would later gather so much expertise on the subject of myeloma that nurses, as well as a few doctors, would mistake him for a medical doctor, not a doctor of theology. This amused him to no end. And he never corrected their misunderstanding. "I get better service," he told me once with a chuckle.)

I hang up the phone and wander into the hall to tell my friends the news. "Dr. Lane has cancer," I say with a vacant expression. It is the beginning of a long road, a hard road, but a road that nonetheless will take us all somewhere we need to go.

~

A few months later, Brenda called and proposed the idea of their moving to Franklin. During the conversation Bill told me why he wanted to spend his last days here. He didn't feel Seattle was home, even after eight years there. Neither did he want to go back to Bowling Green, even though his years there had been some of the happiest of his life. "I want to come to Franklin," he said. "I want to show you how a Christian man dies."

When I hung up the phone from that conversation, I realized through deep sorrow that I had just been given the greatest compliment of my life. There was still more Bill wanted to teach, and for reasons known only to him, he wanted to teach them to me.

In the next year and a half, Bill showed me the truth of great rabbinic writer Abraham Heschel's statement: "For the pious man it is a privilege to die."

*"When the Lord looks me over,
He will not judge me by the degrees
I have earned or the awards I have won,
but by the scars I have incurred."*

After Bill and Brenda decided to move to Franklin, some of his students at Seattle Pacific University proposed a "commissioning service"(rather than a retirement party) for them both as a way to properly send them off to a new arena of ministry. By the Lord's timing, I had a concert in Seattle the day before and secretly planned to stay over in order to attend the event.

I spent the day before the concert following Bill around campus, enjoying being in his considerable shadow once again. We boxed up a few remaining books in his office to prepare for the move. Every book he pulled off the shelf elicited the statement, "Now here is an important volume!" Needless to say, it took twice the time to box up books if he was around!

This particular day was also his last day of class. As we drove to S.P.U. that morning, we both realized that this was, in fact, his final day to teach on a university campus. Needless to say, Bill was nostalgic at the notion of it. And I felt it a tremendous privilege to be with him on that somber morning. There was, understandably, an air of deep sadness as we drove home later that afternoon.

"I feel as if I have not accomplished all that the Lord had for me to do," he mused. He had not finished his "magnum opus," a book on Paul and task theology. Indeed, he would never finish it. He had an obligation to write a commentary on 2 Corinthians, which he was beginning to realize he might not complete as well. The disease, with all its tiredness and aches, was catching up to him, even though he still had more than a year of quality life ahead of him.

I reminded him of one of his favorite sayings, one that he had framed on the wall of his office. Forty years earlier one of his mentors had told him, "When the Lord looks me over, He will not judge me by the degrees I have earned or the awards I have won, but by the scars I have incurred."

That phrase—"the scars I have incurred"—played over and over in my mind as we drove back to his house. I had the feeling of escorting a warrior who was familiar with the scars and tears of the battlefield.

"Everything begins and ends with prayer."

⌒ *A few years before moving to Franklin, Bill had become close to my nephew, Daniel, a sixteen-year-old young man who was engaged in his own battle with cancer. The two of them had talked on the phone and written a few letters back and forth, but now that Bill was essentially in the same town, they would be able to communicate face-to-face.*

By the time he arrived, Bill discovered that Daniel was nearing the end of his struggle; he was constantly in and out of the hospital, trying last-minute, more radical treatments. Bill, himself weak from chemotherapy, would go to visit Daniel whenever he was able. Together the two of them presented a poignant picture. Both men of faith—one older, the other pitifully young—both dealing with their individual ordeals with amazing faith and courage.

The last time I took Bill to see him, Daniel was only

weeks away from dying. He was in the hospital again and had asked if it might be possible for Dr. Lane to visit. As we drove into town, Bill seemed thoughtful.

"This is a dress rehearsal for me," he said.

Even in his weakened condition, when Bill entered the hospital room, both Daniel and my older brother, George, said they could sense the comfort and authority in his presence ("I have the gift of authority," he often said with a smile). He clutched his well-worn Bible in one hand and held Daniel's hand in the other.

They spoke little on this last visit. Bill asked for details about Daniel's condition. By now they were both experts on chemo and its effects.

"I want to share with you a psalm that has helped me enormously" (he loved that word). Opening his Bible to Psalm 91, he read with a passionate voice:

He who dwells in the shelter of the Most High
    will rest in the shadow of the Almighty.
I will say of the LORD, "He is my refuge and my fortress,
    my God, in whom I trust."
Surely he will save you from the fowler's snare
    and from the deadly pestilence.
He will cover you with his feathers,
    and under his wings you will find refuge;
    his faithfulness will be your shield and rampart.

You will not fear the terror of night,
    nor the arrow that flies by day,
nor the pestilence that stalks in the darkness,
    nor the plague that destroys at midday.
A thousand may fall at your side,
    ten thousand at your right hand,
    but it will not come near you.
You will only observe with your eyes
    and see the punishment of the wicked.

If you make the Most High your dwelling—
    even the LORD, who is my refuge—
then no harm will befall you,
    no disaster will come near your tent.
For he will command his angels concerning you
    to guard you in all your ways;
they will lift you up in their hands,
    so that you will not strike your foot against a stone.
You will tread upon the lion and the cobra;
    you will trample the great lion and the serpent.

"Because he loves me," says the LORD, "I will rescue him;
    I will protect him, for he acknowledges my name.
He will call upon me, and I will answer him;
    I will be with him in trouble,
    I will deliver him and honor him.

With long life will I satisfy him
  and show him my salvation."

It seems ironic that Bill found so much comfort in a psalm that speaks of being spared from the deadly pestilence and plague, that talks of surviving in battle when thousands are falling at your side. The psalm promises that no harm will befall you. It promises a long life. Yet Daniel was cut short, and Bill was certainly not an old man at sixty-seven when he died. I believe Bill must have held on to the promise that, even though he and Daniel had not been saved from *their pestilence,* somehow they would be saved through it. They were both that evening in the hospital and most especially now in the shadow of His great wings.

When he was done reading, Bill prayed the most passionate prayer I have heard in my life. He and Daniel were encircled by it. My brother, George, and I stood outside that circle, looking on. Bill cried out for mercy, and he thanked God for the mercy they had both been shown. He pleaded for Daniel's healing, for a miracle, for grace, for courage. He wept and pleaded and dogged God in that prayer. Our hearts were both encouraged and broken by it. We were transported to another place, to the presence of God.

When Bill had finished, he was so weak that my brother had to help him to his feet. As we dried our eyes, Bill said solemnly, "Everything begins and ends with prayer."

A few months later, in November of 1998, barely able to stand because of his own weakness, Bill offered a prayer at Daniel's funeral. He also read his favorite psalm again, for the last time. Bill died two months after the service.

PART IV

Coming Home

Back to Where It All Began

THOUGH JESUS DESIGNATED twelve ordinary men as disciples in Mark, chapter 3, they were not called "apostles" until chapter 6. Their experience of mission with Him had transformed them from disciples to apostles. From "learners" to "the ones who were sent." The latter part of verse 31 captures the essence of the final phase of the cycle of ministry. The disciples reported back all that they had seen and taught, and then they heard Jesus tell them, "Come with me by yourselves to a quiet place and get some rest."

Verse 31 indicates that there had been such an enormous response to their ministry, so many people coming and going, that the disciples did not even have a chance to eat. (You will remember that this was the original reason Mary and Jesus' brothers thought He was out of His mind.) It is another cycle that has come full circle.

Jesus said, "Let's get away." But did they get away? No, in just a few verses we see that the crowd had multiplied to more than five thousand.

Some years ago, I spent five years working toward a one-year sabbatical. The group of pastors who oversee my ministry said, "Okay, if you work hard for these five years, then you'll get an entire year to rest." So for five years, that was the carrot. I worked harder than I ever had before. When the Sabbath year finally arrived, I ended up working harder during that year of "rest" than I had ever worked in my life. So many projects had been put on hold during the intense five years that they all demanded to be finished during what was supposed to be the year of rest. Jesus called me to come away and rest, but when I turned around, the five thousand were there! Can you identify?

But the essence of this final phase of discipleship is more than simply resting, though rest is a crucial element. The real heart of the third phase is sustaining and refreshing our relationship with Jesus. It represents not simply rest but a renewal of relationship, of entering once again into that vital experience of being *with Jesus*. This represents yet another aspect of the cycle coming full circle.

We report back. "Lord, this is what I've done. Lord, these are the things I've said." We share moments with Jesus. After all, we are His commissioned, authoritative representatives. An accounting is due to the One under whose authority we have been ministering.

When was the last time you reported back to Jesus? "This is the work that I'm doing. These are the things I've said. These are the things I've done." If you never have, perhaps it is time for you to hear Jesus say, "Now come with Me and get some rest. Learn from Me in some new situations."

Where are you in this cycle of discipleship? Are you in phase one? Has Jesus called you to be with Him? If so, how long have you been in that phase? Is it not perhaps time for you to hear Jesus say, "Now go and do My work, speak My word"? Or are you stuck in phase two? That's where many of us are. How long have you been there? Is it time for you to hear Jesus say, "Come with Me to a quiet place, get some rest, and learn from Me in some new situations"? Or maybe you've been with Jesus in a quiet place resting. Now it may be time for you to go out and learn once more to be with Jesus.

As I look at this cycle of discipleship and ministry, it's interesting to apply it to the context of each day. I wake in the morning and I'm with Jesus. I learn from Him. I read His Word. I spend time with Him. I realize my commission and then I go out. I do His work and I speak His word. Then at the end of the day, I come back and report to Jesus everything I've done and everything I've said.

Now I hear Him say, "Come with Me to a quiet place and get some rest."

You can apply the cycle over a day, over a matter of months, or over a lifetime. That was my experience with Bill, who first shared this concept with me. After his call and a remarkable period of being with Jesus, he received his commission to speak Jesus' word and do His work. This he faithfully performed for almost forty years. I was with him at the end, when he heard Jesus say, "Come with Me and rest. Be with Me now in new situations. You have no idea of the glory of My Father's presence."

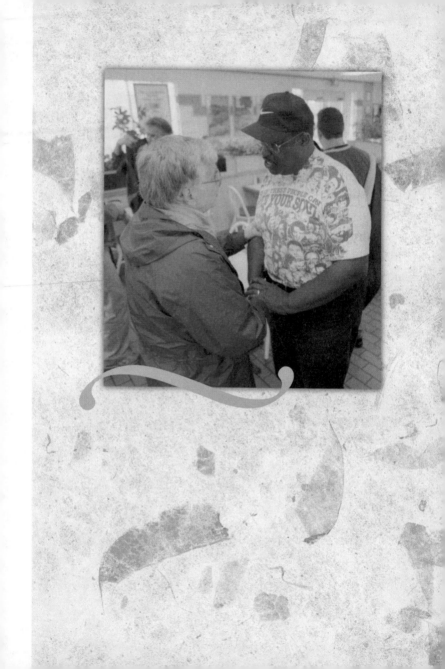

"We are the men of the Empty Hands."

~ We had started meeting a few months before Bill arrived; a motley bunch of pastors, black and white, young and old, to fellowship at McDonald's on Wednesday mornings and to pray at noon on Thursdays. The group didn't begin to focus and solidify until Bill became a member; he became our unspoken leader.

On the first Thursday I introduced Bill to the eight or so men who had come to pray. They knew his story—that he was a celebrated scholar who was dying of cancer. And as you might expect from a group of pastors, they greeted him warmly, welcoming him.

But it was not until Bill began to pray that the brothers met the true person. (The best way to know someone is to listen to them pray.) There was still the authority of his speaking voice, though it had become somewhat hoarse from the cancer's effects. The precision of his language still *shone, but also there was the simple pleading of a child climbing on his Father's lap. There was the persistence he always described as "grabbing hold of the horns of the altar." And there was a deep gratitude that only comes from the person who is able to accept both good and hard times from the hands of God. We had needed someone like Bill. But Bill needed us as well.*

"I am amazed at how completely I have been accepted by you men," he said once to a group of us. That may sound a bit confusing, given the circumstances. Why shouldn't we be thrilled at having such a person as Bill in our midst? But the fact is, he had not always been so warmly received and accepted. Often he had been greeted with professional jealousy, which had wounded him deeply. But now, in the last months of his life, Bill felt warmly enfolded into a community that both admired him and welcomed him to lean into them for the support he so badly needed.

Looking at Bill for the Last Time

〜 On January 15, 1999, we celebrated Bill and Brenda's one-year anniversary of being in Franklin. The best way to describe the party was raucous. Pastors from the Empty Hands and their wives, students who had studied with Bill at the Franklin House—all crammed into the study center to celebrate his life. In a few months he would be gone.

Brenda and I planned a "birthday" party then, even though his birthday was months away, since we knew he was getting worse and might be too sick to celebrate on the actual day. We served his favorite dessert, "Brown Derbys," a glazed donut with a scoop of vanilla ice cream on top, all covered with lots of hot chocolate sauce.

Afterward I told Bill, "I'm glad we did this now," only realizing after I said it that I'd implied he was running out of time.

"Don't worry about it," Bill said, still aglow from the party. *"None of us ever knows when our time will come."*

～

It is two months later now. I'm sitting in what will become the central classroom of the study center. At this moment it is still their living room. I'm holding Bill's hand as he lies dying. His time has come.

I look at his hand, the familiar ring. I remember seeing him gesture as he would lecture. His breathing is labored and starting to slow down. Soon he will be gone. "When does it cease to be his hand?" I ask myself. Bill would be the first person I'd ask such a question, if he were able to answer me now. Is this the first time I've ever really seen that hand? I look at my own hand and wait for him to "fall asleep."

Like most great truths, it is a paradox: In order to really see something for the first time, it must be as if you are looking at it for the last time. But this will not be the last time, if what my faith tells me is correct. I will see Bill and this hand again, I will hear that booming voice over the multitude, singing praise to God. "Look, beaaautiful!"

Unfinished Business

⌒ *In preparing to write this book, I worked through a file of newspaper articles about Bill. In many of them he talked to the reporter about a book he had been working on for years. In a newspaper article dated 7 June 1981, the writer stated that after Bill returned from a sabbatical at Cambridge, he would "begin work on a major volume on the apostle Paul which has been germinating for 10 or 15 years."* His working title was Apostle and Task Theologian: Paul in the Perspective of Mission.

His "magnum opus," his "big one." That was Bill's way of referring to the major work on Paul, which he had been researching for decades. Though he had written major commentaries on the books of Mark and Hebrews, it was primarily the life of Paul that dominated his interest and his amazing mind.

Often in the middle of a discussion on Paul, we would

have to stop Bill and say, "This is still Paul we're talking about?" We would ask this half jokingly but also half seriously because his conversation had started to sound like he was discussing a close colleague or friend. He knew the mind and heart of Paul as perhaps few ever have.

A typical exchange would go something like this:

"It was during this missionary journey that Paul contracted malaria," Bill would say with the utmost confidence.

"But how could you possibly know that?" someone would respond.

"Because this is a very swampy area, known for malaria-infested mosquitoes," Bill would reply, "and it was only after this point in his ministry that Paul began to speak of the thorn in his flesh." And somehow it would all make sense.

Bill dubbed his unique category for approaching the letters of Paul as "task theology." His theory was that in order to understand Paul, you must take seriously the fact that he was first and foremost a missionary, and he shaped his theology to suit his particular missionary task. It is vital to understand that Paul was always addressing a particular life situation on the mission field. The failure to understand this accounts for so much misunderstanding and dissension in the area of Pauline studies.

The question from Brenda that shocked Bill into the awareness that he had only a limited amount of time left was, "Who do you want me to get to finish your book on Paul when you die?" That question eventually led him to come to Franklin. His hope was that here he would finally be able to focus on Paul exclusively and finish the book. But there was simply not enough time.

There was not enough time . . . What does a statement like that imply? Did God make a mistake in his allotment of time to Bill? Had Bill, a man who worked almost sinfully hard, wasted the time he had been given? Or is there another lesson to be learned?

Behind every specific call, whether it is to teach or preach or write or encourage or comfort, there is a deeper call that gives shape to the first: the call to give ourselves away—the call to die. We can, in an incomplete way, give ourselves by writing books or sermons or even songs, but it will always be a fragmentary and incomplete giving because these tasks require no real personal contact.

But real contact was what Bill was all about, and throughout his life he was torn between the academic call—to cloister himself within the library in order to write articles and books—and opening the door of his life to real, living, breathing people who needed his gifts. Ultimately, by grace, he listened to the deeper call to give himself intimately to his family and friends and students, and as a direct result, what he called his magnum opus will never be finished.

Before Bill and Brenda left Seattle to come to Tennessee, the chaplain of the university held a commissioning service for both of them to send them off to a new area of ministry in Franklin. At that service, Bill's students and friends were invited to share encouraging words with the Lanes before they left. In the midst of all that encouragement, one of Bill's "boys" shocked us all by what he said.

"Everyone has been recounting all of your qualities, Bill," he said to the crowd. "But I would like to mention something that is wrong with you. You have trouble finishing your work!" A slight gasp came up from the audience. There was a moment of tense silence. Then Bill's friend continued, "And we would like to thank you for not finishing it. For if you had spent the time required to complete the book on Paul, you would not have had the time to invest in us . . . We are your books, Bill!" It was the kind of powerful moment that only the stating of a self-evident truth can bring.

While the call may be to write books or sermons or poems, the deeper call will always be to give ourselves away to others whom God places within our reach. Besides a few words scribbled in the sand, as far as we know, Jesus never wrote a single line. Instead He wrote the Living

Word across the pages of those twelve unlikely men who changed the world. So, despite any evidence to the contrary, Bill wonderfully finished his "business." And what will always be left unfinished about it, we are called to complete!

The Final Good-bye

~ We were coming closer to the end of our walk *together, and we both knew it. When I came to pick Bill up for our weekly morning breakfast at McDonald's with the men of the Empty Hands Fellowship (he had come up with the name), he finally broke down and accepted the step stool that I always offered him to help him climb into my Land Cruiser. He used to turn it down by saying something like, "I'm not that bad off yet." But now he was beginning to be that bad off, and we both knew it.*

As we drove the short two blocks to meet with the brothers, he brought up the subject of his memorial service. He spoke of it often, going over and over the details, occasionally changing them.

"I'm not ready to talk about this now," I said, keeping my eyes focused straight ahead. And it was true. I had heard his list before. I believed I had enough of a picture of what

he wanted. And that morning, after seeing his frailty climbing into the jeep, I didn't want to hear any more. I simply wasn't ready.

"Well, you'd better get ready!" he said almost harshly.

Then after a brief pause, he proceeded. "You know about the shock of wheat for the casket?"

"Yes."

"And I want to be buried in the black section of Mount Hope."

"Yes, I know. Brenda is looking into that." I tried to think of something humorous to say about the possibility of Bill not being allowed into the black area of the cemetery, something that might lighten the moment, but nothing came.

When we arrived at the parking lot, Bill put his hand on mine and whispered, "The symptoms associated with the final phase of my myeloma have begun. My vision is becoming cloudy, like looking through a spider web. I'm having nosebleeds that won't stop. And, Michael, I am beginning to experience the bone pain. I don't know if I can handle it."

Bill was as courageous a man as I had ever known. I have seen pictures of him preaching on the streets at Mardi Gras, when he was accosted by a group of Hell's Angels. "If I slapped you in the face, would you turn the other cheek?" a burly biker had said as he prodded Bill from the crowd.

"Yes," Bill responded. "Look around you. People are in conversation, and I wouldn't do anything to disrupt that."

Then the man drew a line with his foot, warning Bill that if he crossed it he would "knock him down."

Bill stepped across the line, fully expecting to be punched. But he had to show the crowd of young students that he was unwilling to be silenced from speaking for Christ because of this one man. As he moved within reach of the biker, there was a moment of tense silence. Then all at once the man erupted, "You're all right." He patted Bill on the back and disappeared into the crowd.

Bill had preached on the streets in Amsterdam, carrying a cross and experiencing such hostility from the crowd that he later said he believed he understood better what Jesus had experienced on the way to Calvary. He was as courageous a man as I have ever known, but in the face of the kind of suffering that he knew awaited him, he wondered, "I don't know if I'm ready for this." He had never looked so frail and afraid as that moment in the parking lot.

We had one earlier scare at McDonald's. He had become dizzy and asked me to help him home. Once there, Denny Denson, Mike Smith, and I carried him to the couch in his apartment at the Franklin House. It seemed that this was it. He was somewhat incoherent yet still aware that we were there around him. We all begged him to go to the hospital, but it was Brenda who realized that if this was the end, he wanted to experience it at home.

We helped him into bed and waited in the living room

as he and Brenda cuddled together, saying their good-byes.

After awhile she came out of the bedroom. I was certain that she would say he had died. But instead she told us he had fallen asleep. He had taken his blood pressure medicine on an empty stomach, which explains why we could not feel a pulse. In a few hours he was up and feeling fine.

What struck me about that first scare was his demeanor through it all. He was laughing, not from dizziness or disorientation, but from some sort of joy that is probably beyond the ability of most of us to understand.

Three weeks after that final day at McDonald's, Bill was taken to the hospital after an initial stroke that occurred at 5:00 Friday morning. He fell asleep and essentially never woke up. It was decided to bring him home if he could survive being taken off the respirator. He actually improved after he was disconnected from all the machines. I remembered his dismay the first time he had ever been unconscious, awaking with a catheter, saying, "I feel violated." I wondered now what he would say with a machine doing his breathing for him.

The last night we slept in shifts. Brenda, who was completely exhausted, Bill's daughter, Kris, and I stayed with him. Kris sat with him first, waking me to help with turning him. I slept on an army cot in the Old Testament room of the Franklin House library, surrounded by floor-to-ceiling bookcases filled with his books (five thousand are housed in *the two rooms of the library), while he lay dying in the next room.*

When the ambulance that brought him home from the hospital arrived, I asked if I might help carry him into the house. Two days later, after he died, I helped carry his body to the hearse that had come from the funeral home to pick him up. Then two days later, his sons would honor me by inviting me to help carry the casket from the hearse to the gravesite.

Three relatively simple sounding tasks, yet to put into words what they mean to me is impossible. In one sense, Bill had been carrying me for so many years; it was a wonderful parable, this last token of being allowed to carry him.

Abraham Heschel, the well-known Jewish author and rabbi, quoted a Hasidic tradition:

"There are three ascending levels of how one mourns; with tears—that is the lowest. With silence—that is higher. And with a song—that is the highest."

I passed freely through the first level shortly after Bill died. This book is a result of the second level, as I listened to the silence of all our years together. I still wait, with great expectation, to mourn my beloved mentor with a song.

The Dirty Little Secret

As I sit at my desk, trying to finish this manuscript, I am surrounded by death. Just yesterday one of my best friends, Hyndman, passed away in a hospital in Belfast. One minute he was joking with a nurse named Margarita, the next, as she turned around to laugh, he was gone. He was not simply a man who introduced me to Ireland. He was the brother who also opened up an entire world for me, a world he taught that was impregnated with joy.

As we prepare for a service for him on this side of the cold Atlantic, I have pulled out all of my pictures of him. They are scattered in a loose pile on one side of the desk. Next to that pile is a folder full of pictures of Bill for this book. Beside both of these is a framed picture of my eighteen-year-old nephew, Daniel, who died a few months before Bill. He's holding a guitar I gave him and smiling a wonderfully alive sort of smile. Above him on the wall is a picture of my grandfather F. F. Brown, who died when I was two and whom I would have given almost anything to have known. For me right now, death is everywhere I look.

Malcolm Muggeridge, the British commentator and apologist who was so preoccupied with the topic of death (particularly his own), said in one of his later books that in our time it is no longer sex that is the "dirty little secret"; it has become death. Though we all know of the fact and inevitability of death, we live in a world that functions as if it did not exist at all, in a world where people act as if they will live forever. It is no wonder then that when death comes, we seem surprised.

But there is a deeper reason for our difficulty in dealing with death. During the funeral service of an eight-year-old girl who had been tragically killed in an auto accident, my friend Mike Smith spoke the only words I heard that morning that made sense of the confusion and senselessness of death. He tearfully said simply, "We were not created for this."

That's it! We were created for more, for better, for eternal life. At the core of our being something deep, pre-existent, revolts at the thought of life ending, of it being snuffed out by something as trivial and impotent as disease or accident or old age.

Bill used to speak of a "death-impregnated world," of a world so deeply impacted by the Fall that death colors every aspect of our lives. It was one of his "categories," a feature of the grid he sought to pass on to us. One of the greatest gifts a mentor can pass on to a disciple is a value system founded on God's Word, a matrix through which we see and understand and seek to make sense of the otherwise confusing and senseless fallen world. As Bill would say, "We must make a place in the system for death, the last enemy" (1 Cor. 15:26).

In those last days he frequently spoke of death as the enemy, as something against which he was engaged in battle. On Sunday, March 7, 1999, Bill lost that battle. Or did he?

In John 5:24, Jesus promised that if we hear His Word and believe in Him, we will have already crossed over from death to life. From Jesus' point of view, all who do not know Him are already dead. His Word wakes those who are the living-dead into new Life. That, quite simply, is where death fit into Jesus' value system. Whenever He faced literal death, whether it was the death of His good friend Lazarus in John 11:11 or the little girl who died in Mark 5:39, Jesus always referred to death as "sleep," as something from which we will be awakened by Him.

A friend of mine received great comfort from Michael Podesta's words on one of his popular cards:

IMAGINE

Stepping onto a shore and finding it heaven

IMAGINE

taking hold of a hand and finding it God's hand

IMAGINE

breathing new air and finding it celestial air

IMAGINE

feeling invigorated and finding it immortality

IMAGINE

passing from storm and tempest to an unknown calm

IMAGINE

waking and finding it home.

Such a comforting idea! But as we stand beside the casket and look upon the face of a friend, or even as we look into the mirror at our own dying faces, the death-impregnated world's theory seems much more realistic: Death is final, it is inescapable, and so perhaps it is best kept a secret.

Jesus' value system is the more difficult to embrace, given what seem to be the painful realities of death. His position can be embraced only by the foolishness we call faith; it can be held onto only by the delicate empowering of His Spirit. And so, I hereby choose to believe that the friends in the pictures on my desk are at this moment more alive than those who, though living, do not know Christ.

Bill had said, "I want to show you how a Christian man dies." I have only recently realized that this lesson began the first moment we met. It continued for twenty years or more, because each time I was within Bill's reach, I was being powerfully taught or even more powerfully shown the *life* of faith and Spirit. And it is that life that best prepares us for the slumber Jesus spoke about.

And so, I look intently at the pictures of my friends who have fallen asleep. In their pictures they are laughing, mugging before the camera on perfect summer days that will soon be forgotten. They are dead to the world now, but nevertheless alive in God's presence. That is my secret—it is neither little nor is it dirty, and I must share it with all the dead men and women and boys and girls who surround me in this death-impregnated world.

Tears

~ Since Bill's death I find something has happened to me that he had said happened to him in his last days. We would be talking about the past or perhaps the worsening condition of my nephew, and all of a sudden tears would come to his eyes. "I am becoming more tenderhearted," he would say as he wiped them away.

Tears seem to stay closer to the surface for me as well these days. They will come, unbidden, in the midst of prayer. Sometimes I'm not even aware that they are there until I feel them on my cheek.

Sorrow is a burden any way you look at it. It seems there are only two things it can do to us, or we can do with it: First, sorrow can bear down on us, causing us to crack and break, which is not a completely bad thing. Brokenness is a vital companion on the walk.

Second, the sorrow can settle down somewhere deep

inside us and solidify. Then it becomes like the ballast in a ship, the weight that keeps the ship upright even in the fiercest storm.

I'm not sure which of these is happening in me—perhaps some of both, or maybe something to which I cannot put words. I don't know. But I believe in tears and the purpose of pain.

The Lord bestowed on me (and all of us who walked with Bill) a wonderful gift. When God gives us a gift, He does wrap it in a person. Sometimes we don't see the true value of a gift until it's gone. In missing it we discover how dear it was to us.

Reaching Outward and Upward

~ As I packed up my notes and letters and pictures upon the completion of this manuscript, I came across a small black-and-white picture I had not noticed before. It had been torn out of a photo album, by the looks of it. The picture is of a small boy of perhaps two or three years of age. He has a "Buster Brown" haircut and is sporting a one-piece white playsuit. His expression is unusually intense for a child of his years.

His left hand is extended outward and upward. It's hard to tell what this gesture means exactly. Is he pointing to something, to a bird perhaps, anxious that those around him not miss the sight of it? He seems concerned that the photographer is missing something more important that is going on behind him. I can almost hear his small voice, "Look, wooonderful!"

Or is he reaching for something, maybe a flower? "Beaaautiful!"

On the back of the photograph, scrawled in pencil I read, "Billy Lane, Jr., August 193 . . . " A flake of glue from the forgotten album obscures the last number of the year.

Without reading the back of the picture, I know, of course, who it is a picture of. Though the face and expression are vaguely familiar, that is not what gives the little boy away. The left-handedness provides a good clue, though an inconclusive one. It is the manner of the reaching that tells me who it is. It says, "Look! Don't miss this . . . It is wonderful . . . It is beautiful."

When Bill was reaching for an idea, reaching out to us, in the classroom, he often made this gesture. When we would take hikes in the mountains, he was forever doing this. As I look back on other pictures of him, most often he is pointing, reaching for something: a petroglyph, a bluebird, a leaf, a flower, an idea, or most often a person.

That little boy reached out to me for the first time on a perfect fall morning. Again and again he would reach out to encourage or to instruct. He lived out the gospel for me. Essentially because of him I now believe that it truly is "good news." From that first moment, regardless of what he was pointing at or pointing out, he was always pointing to Jesus. Through his faults and foibles as much as his incredible genius, Bill made Jesus come alive in my life. And is that not what we are all called to do?

Invariably this mystical experience would take place in the context of that most mundane of experiences, a walk.

A Funeral Prayer

BY WILLIAM LANE

ALMIGHTY GOD, LORD of Life and Conqueror over death, our help in every time of trouble: Breathe Thy peace into our hearts, and remove from us all fear of death. Help us to share in that joy which Thou dost have in the death of Thy saints, who have completed their pilgrimage through a world which was not their home and have entered into a more intimate fellowship with Thee. Strengthen us in our sorrow, and enable us so to hear Thy holy Word, that through patience and the comfort of the Scriptures our hope may be firmly anchored. And grant us the consolation of Thy Holy Spirit, that we may be lifted above the shadows of mortality into the light of Thy countenance and the joy of Thy presence; through Him who died and rose again and ever liveth with Thee, even Jesus Christ.

Appendix

Bill's Statement of Faith in Christ

In Jesus Christ, God's grace is expressed in its sharpest detail. God Himself, veiled in human flesh, penetrates the world to address men and women one final time. By this act of God I am brought face to face with the reality and the mystery of the Incarnation. He who stands over against us, as wholly other than ourselves—for God is not man—comes to stand with us as the Man wholly for others. In the Man, Christ Jesus, God is in the world atoning for our sins.

The purpose of the Incarnation was to redeem and reconcile men and women. By His perfect obedience to the Father, both during His earthly ministry and in submitting to death on behalf of the community of faith, Jesus satisfied God's judging righteousness and turned away God's wrath. Because Jesus willingly identified Himself with us, assuming upon Himself the judgment upon sin which we had merited, God is able to display His saving righteousness, to be appropriated through faith.

Jesus' cross, resurrection, and ascension form a single complex through which He was exalted to the Father's presence, where He now functions as King and Priest. As King He must reign until all His enemies, including death, are destroyed. As Priest He intercedes on behalf of His people. I believe He will return in triumphant splendor to judge the living and the dead. Then faith will be exchanged for sight, and all Christians will experience the unmediated presence of God in Jesus Christ their Lord.

About the Author

⁓ Michael Card is a popular Christian songwriter, recording artist, and author. Anyone who is familiar with Card's music has relished his ability to weave a story with word and melody. For almost two decades his biblically based recordings have brought to life Scripture's most enigmatic characters and unraveled its most difficult texts. Since his 1981 debut album, *First Light,* Card has used his knowledge of the Scriptures to create musical word pictures that spark the imagination and rekindle lagging faith.

Michael holds an undergraduate and a master's degree in Biblical Studies from Western Kentucky University. His musical journey began when he wrote a song as a favor to his pastor while he was working on his master's degree. In the years since then, he has penned some of Christian music's most cherished songs, including "El-Shaddai." He has released twenty recordings and has authored or coauthored twelve books, including *A Violent Grace, The Parable of Joy,* and *Joy in the Journey.* Collectively, his works have sold more than four million copies. Card has earned five Dove Awards, and nineteen of his songs have reached number one on Christian radio charts.

Card was nominated for the C. S. Lewis Children's Book Award for *Sleep Sound in Jesus,* which was also a finalist for the Evangelical Christian Publishers Association's Gold Medallion Award.

Though awards and recognition are always welcome affirmation of any artist's work, this is not Card's motivation. He says, "The purpose of my music, books, and concerts is to focus in on and worship Christ. The songs and writings are just vehicles to accomplish this purpose."

Michael and his wife, Susan, have four children and live in Franklin, Tennessee.